America the Beautiful

Landscapes, Symbols, and Citizens of Our Nation

ISBN: 978-1-59577-083-7

Starfall Education

P.O. Box 359, Boulder, Colorado 80306

O beautiful

Mountain Pastures

For spacious skies,

Wheat Fields

For amber waves of grain,

Rocky Mountains, CO

For purple mountain majesties

Apple Orchard

Above the fruited plain!

Grape Vineyard

Independence Hall
Philadelphia, PA

Liberty Bell
Philadelphia, PA

America!

U.S. Capital
Washington, DC

Mount Rushmore
SD

The Marine Corps War Memorial
Arlington, VA

America!

The White House
Washington, DC

Everglades, FL

God shed His grace on thee,

Canyon Country, UT

And crown thy good

Statue of Liberty, NY

American Children

With brotherhood

From sea...

Pacific Coast

to shining sea!

Atlantic Coast

Pike's Peak, CO

America the Beautiful is a poem by Katharine Lee Bates, written in the summer of 1893 after visiting Colorado Springs.

"One day some of the other teachers and I decided to go on a trip to 14,000 foot Pike's Peak. We hired a prairie wagon. Near the top we had to leave the wagon and go the rest of the way on mules. I was very tired. But when I saw the view, I felt great joy. All the wonder of America seemed displayed there, with the sea like expanse."

– *Katharine Lee Bates*

Music by: Samuel Augustus Ward

America the Beautiful

Lyrics by: Katharine Lee Bates

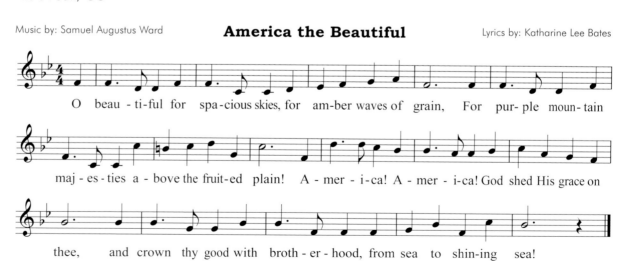

O beau-ti-ful for spa-cious skies, for am-ber waves of grain, For pur-ple moun-tain

maj - es - ties a - bove the fruit-ed plain! A - mer - i-ca! A - mer - i-ca! God shed His grace on

thee, and crown thy good with broth - er - hood, from sea to shin-ing sea!